THE CHANGING CLIMATE OF

ANTARCTICA

Patricia K. Kummer

NORTH AMERICA

SOUTH AMERICA

EUROPE

ASIA

AFRICA

AUSTRALIA

Cavendish Square

New York

ANTARCTICA

Published in 2014 by Cavendish Square Publishing, LLC

303 Park Avenue South, Suite 1247, New York, NY 10010

Copyright © 2014 by Cavendish Square Publishing, LLC

First Edition

Website: cavendishsq.com

This publication represents the opinions and views of the author based on his or her personal experience, knowledge, and research. The information in this book serves as a general guide only. The author and publisher have used their best efforts in preparing this book and disclaim liability rising directly or indirectly from the use and application of this book.

CPSIA Compliance Information: Batch #WW14CSQ

All websites were available and accurate when this book was sent to press.

Library of Congress Cataloging-in-Publication Data
Kummer, Patricia K.
The changing climate of Antarctica / by Patricia K. Kummer.
p. cm. — (Climates and continents)
Summary: "Provides comprehensive information on the geography, wildlife, peoples, and climate of the continent of Antarctica and the changes taking place there as a result of climate change"—Provided by publisher. Includes index.
ISBN 978-1-62712-440-9 (hardcover) ISBN 978-1-62712-441-6 (paperback) ISBN 978-1-62712-442-3 (ebook)
1. Climatic changes — Environmental aspects — Antarctica. I. Kummer, Patricia K. II. Title.
QH84.2 K86 2014
577.5—dc23

Editorial Director: Dean Miller
Senior Editor: Peter Mavrikis
Copy Editor: Cynthia Roby
Art Director: Jeffrey Talbot
Designer: Amy Greenan
Photo Researcher: Alison Morretta
Production Manager: Jennifer Ryder-Talbot
Production Editor: Andrew Coddington

The photographs in this book are used by permission and through the courtesy of: Cover photo by PT1/WENN.com/Newscom; Davor Puk-ljak/Shutterstock.com, 4; Mapping Specialists, 6; Cliff Leight/Aurora/Getty Images, 9; Dorling Kindersley/Getty Images, 10; Higdon Photo-graphic Art Studio/SuperStock, 12; NASA/Science Faction/SuperStock, 14; Mapping Specialists, 15; Cliff Leight/Aurora/Getty Images, 16; Thomas Pickard/Aurora/Getty Images, 17; Minden Pictures/SuperStock, 18; Carsten Peter/National Geographic/Getty Images, 21; Doug Allan/The Image Bank/Getty Images, 23; Maria Stenzel/National Geographic/Getty Images, 25; Steve Bloom Images/SuperStock, 26; Carsten Peter/National Geographic/Getty Images, 27; Ralph Lee Hopkins/Lonely Planet Images/Getty Images, 29; GILLARDI Jacques/he-mis.fr/Getty Images, 29; Sue Flood/The Image Bank/Getty Images, 30; Danita Delimont/Gallo Images/Getty Images, 32; Colin Monteath/ago footstock/Getty Images, 33; Biosphoto/SuperStock, 35; Hubertus Kanus/Photo researchers/Getty Images, 37; Norbert Wu/Science Faction/SuperStock, 38; NASA/Science Faction/SuperStock, 40; AP Photo/R. Robert, International Polar Foundation, 42.

Printed in the United States of America

CONTENTS

ONE

THE SOUTHERNMOST CONTINENT

Looking at a globe or at a world map, it is quite easy to identify the seven **continents**. They are Earth's largest land areas. Antarctica is the third-smallest continent. It covers about 9 percent of Earth's land. Europe and Australia are smaller continents. The other five continents in order of size are Asia, Africa, North America, and South America.

Getting To Know Antarctica

Antarctica is the southernmost of the continents. It is at the bottom of the world where the geographic South Pole marks the southernmost point on Earth. The Transantarctic Mountain Range unequally divides the continent into two regions—East Antarctica and West Antarctica. The geographic South Pole, which also marks the center of Antarctica, lies about 200 miles (322 km) east of the mountains.

The large white area in this satellite image is the continent of Antarctica, which is almost completely covered with snow and ice.

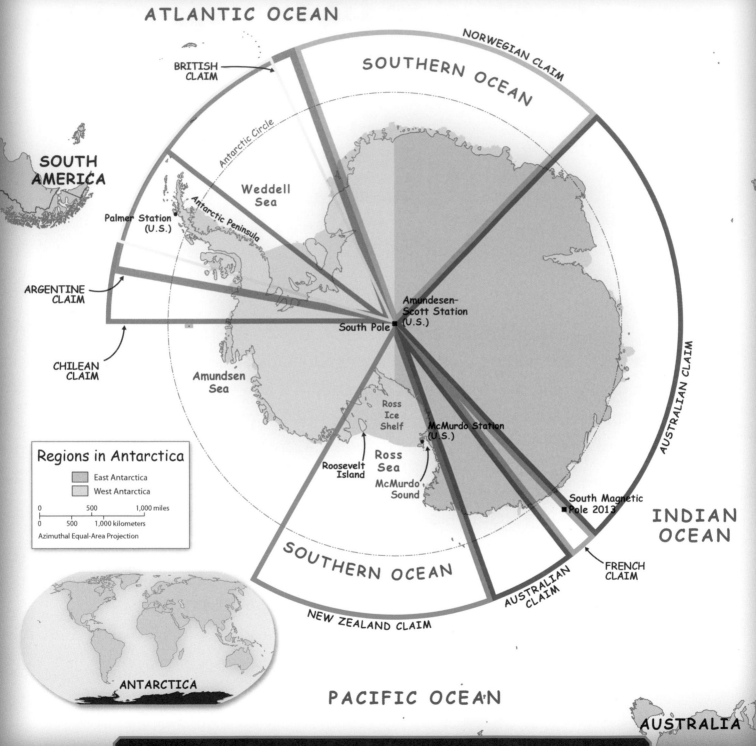

ATLANTIC OCEAN

NORWEGIAN CLAIM

SOUTHERN OCEAN

BRITISH CLAIM

SOUTH AMERICA

Antarctic Circle

Weddell Sea

Palmer Station (U.S.)

Antarctic Peninsula

ARGENTINE CLAIM

Amundesen–Scott Station (U.S.)

South Pole

CHILEAN CLAIM

Amundsen Sea

AUSTRALIAN CLAIM

Ross Ice Shelf

McMurdo Station (U.S.)

Roosevelt Island

Ross Sea

McMurdo Sound

South Magnetic Pole 2013

INDIAN OCEAN

Regions in Antarctica

East Antarctica

West Antarctica

0   500   1,000 miles
0   500   1,000 kilometers

Azimuthal Equal-Area Projection

SOUTHERN OCEAN

FRENCH CLAIM

AUSTRALIAN CLAIM

NEW ZEALAND CLAIM

ANTARCTICA

PACIFIC OCEAN

AUSTRALIA

POLITICAL MAP OF ANTARCTICA

Where in the World Is Antarctica?

MAPPING SKILLS

Use the political map on page 6 to answer the following questions about the continent of Antarctica:

1. Which continent is Antarctica's closest neighbor? About how many miles away is it?

2. Which ocean completely surrounds Antarctica?

3. Which region in Antarctica is the largest one?

4. Which country has the largest land claim in East Antarctica? Why do you think that occurred?

5. Which three countries have overlapping claims in West Antarctica?

6. Name the three research stations owned by the United States.

ANSWERS:
1. South America; about 600 miles (965 km)
2. Southern Ocean
3. East Antarctica
4. Australia; It's the closest country/continent to that part of Antarctica.
5. Argentina, Britain, Chile
6. Amundsen-Scott, McMurdo, and Palmer

Antarctica lies almost completely within the Antarctic Circle. This location gives the entire continent a cold, dry polar climate. Thick **ice sheets** and **glaciers** cover Antarctica's land. This polar climate and icy land support few species of plants and animals. Their main **habitats** are Antarctica's coast and the Southern Ocean. This ocean completely surrounds the continent.

Seven countries—Argentina, Australia, Chile, France, New Zealand, Norway, and the United Kingdom—have claimed parts of Antarctica. However, Antarctica is the only continent that is not divided into countries. Instead, the continent is protected by fifty countries that have signed the Antarctic Treaty. Those countries agree to pursue only peaceful, scientific research in Antarctica. More than twenty countries have established research stations on the continent. Scientists from those countries study Antarctica's climate, weather, air quality, land, and plants and animals.

Antarctica is also the only continent that has no indigenous (native) people. In addition, no permanent population lives there today. During the summer, a few thousand people live and work at the research stations. Tourists also come ashore for short visits. During the winter, some research stations close down completely.

The Changing Continents

For hundreds of millions of years, Antarctica and the other continents have undergone slow, continuous change. In fact about 250 million

The Geographic South Pole

The geographic South Pole is about in the middle of Antarctica. This is the southern point where Earth rotates on its axis. A long steel rod, pushed deep into the ice, marks the location of the South Pole. Every year on New Year's Day, a special ceremony takes place. Scientists from the nearby US Amundsen-Scott South Pole Station place a new rod in another spot. No, the South Pole isn't moving. Instead, the ice on top of Antarctica moves about 30 feet (9 meters) every year.

years ago, there was only one continent—Pangaea. Gradually, Pangaea broke apart. About 100 million years ago, Antarctica reached its current location. At that time, Antarctica was still attached to Australia and to South America. About 50 million years ago, Australia pulled away from Antarctica. South America pulled away about 35 million years ago. Then, Antarctica was alone at the bottom of the world.

At that time, the **Antarctic Circumpolar Current** (ACC) formed in the Southern Ocean. The ACC flows west to east around Antarctica. It is the only current that flows all around the world. The ACC is a cold ocean current. It prevents warm waters from the Atlantic, Indian, and Pacific oceans from reaching Antarctica. The ACC helped the continent's ice sheet to form. By 14 million years ago, ice sheets covered the entire continent. Today, the ACC helps Antarctica maintain its ice sheets.

Each of Earth's continents sits on a **tectonic plate**. Antarctica is in the middle of the Antarctic Plate. The hard, rigid sheets of rock are always moving. Tectonic

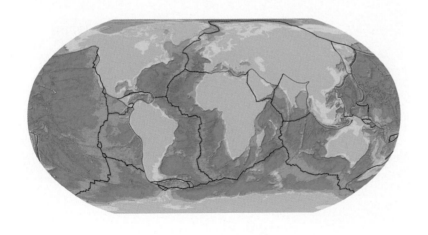

This map shows Earth's tectonic plates.

movement causes the continents' locations to change. Each year, Antarctica creeps less than one-half inch (1 cm) toward the Atlantic Ocean. Tectonic movement also pushes up mountains, such as the Transantarctic Mountains. Volcanoes such as the ones on Ross Island are the products of tectonic movement, too.

Earthquakes and **tsunamis** are other tectonic events. Even when they occur on other continents, they can affect Antarctica. In March 2011, a powerful earthquake shook Japan's Honshu Island. When the earthquake's shock waves reached Antarctica, they caused the flow of the Whillans Glacier to speed up. Then, the tsunami that followed the earthquake hit Antarctica. Its waves broke **icebergs** from the Sulzberger Ice Shelf.

Continents and Climate Change

Another change that concerns Antarctica and the other continents is **climate change**. The main cause of climate change is the release of large amounts of certain gases into the air. The most threatening gases are carbon dioxide (CO_2), **chlorofluorocarbons** (CFCs), and **methane**. Natural events such as volcanic eruptions add small amounts of CO_2 to the air. Human activities such as burning coal, oil, natural gas, and gasoline emit large amounts of CO_2. Aerosol sprays and coolants for refrigerators and air conditioners give off CFCs. Decaying plants, garbage, and animal waste create methane.

When this piece of the Ross Ice Shelf breaks off, it will be an iceberg floating in the ocean.

Increased emissions of these gases have caused global temperatures to rise. They have also caused more precipitation (rain and snow) to fall in some places and less in others. Even in unpopulated Antarctica, climate change has occurred. The activities of people on other continents are responsible for those changes. CFC emissions have caused thinning of the **ozone layer** over Antarctica. In 1985, British scientists in Antarctica brought this problem to the world's attention. Now, people throughout the world are trying to change their habits. Some improvements have already occurred, which will lead to still more change.

TWO

THE HIGHEST, ICIEST LAND

Ice sheets and glaciers cover at least 98 percent of Antarctica's rocky land. These thick layers of ice formed because Antarctica's cold temperatures prevented snow from melting. Mountains, plateaus, and valleys lie under the ice. In some places, the ice can be more than 10,560 feet (3,219 m) thick. Land along the Antarctic Peninsula and on nearby islands has the least ice cover.

Antarctica is also the highest continent. The average elevation of the land under the ice is at least 7,500 feet (2,300 m) above sea level. About 50 mountain peaks stand more than 12,000 feet (3,660 m) above sea level. Only the tops of those peaks poke through the ice sheets.

The Transantarctic Mountains stretch across the continent. Some peaks reach heights of more than 14,800 feet (4,511 m) above sea level.

Mountains and Plateaus

The Transantarctic Mountains divide the continent into East Antarctica and West Antarctica. Those mountains had formed before Antarctica was covered with ice. Because of that, each part of Antarctica has its own ice sheet. East Antarctica's ice sheet is older, larger, and thicker.

Small groups of mountains rise near East Antarctica's coast. Inland, the high Antarctic Plateau covers much of East Antarctica. Most of the plateau stands 10,000 feet (3,000 m) above sea level. At this elevation, the air is colder and thinner than at lower elevations near the coast. These conditions make it difficult to breathe.

West Antarctica has the continent's extreme elevations. In the Ellsworth Mountains, the Vinson Massif stands 16,066 feet (4,897 m) above sea level. The Bentley Subglacial Trench lies 8,327 feet (2,538 m) below sea level. The weight of the West Antarctica ice sheet has pushed the land down into this trench. West Antarctica also has Earth's driest land—the Dry Valleys. These valleys of bare rock lie between the

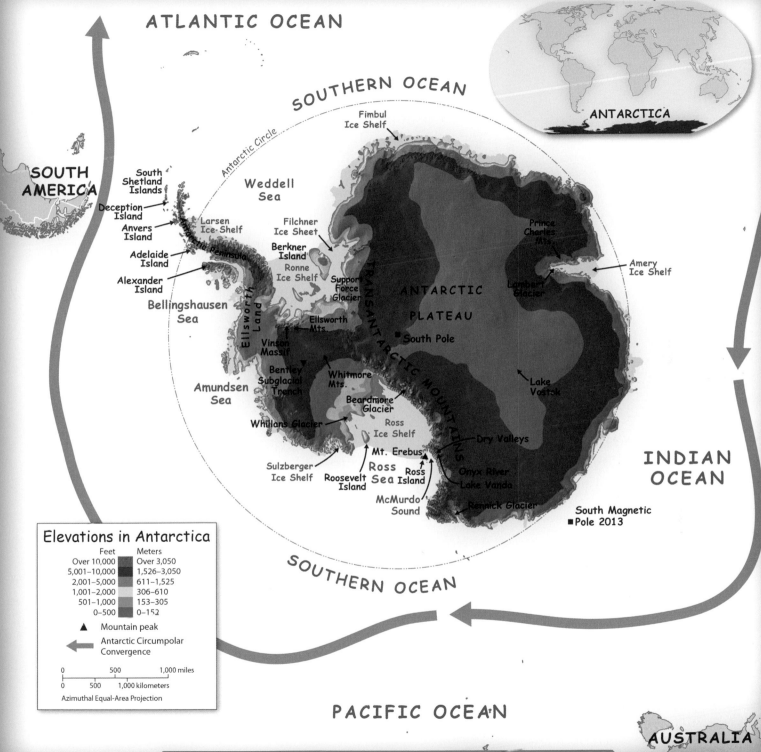

ATLANTIC OCEAN

SOUTHERN OCEAN

ANTARCTICA

SOUTH AMERICA

Antarctic Circle

Fimbul Ice Shelf

South Shetland Islands

Weddell Sea

Deception Island

Larsen Ice Shelf

Anvers Island

Filchner Ice Sheet

Prince Charles Mts

Adelaide Island

Berkner Island

Antarctic Peninsula

Amery Ice Shelf

Alexander Island

Ronne Ice Shelf

Support Force Glacier

Lambert Glacier

Bellingshausen Sea

ANTARCTIC PLATEAU

Ellsworth Land

Ellsworth Mts.

South Pole

Vinson Massif

Lake Vostok

Bentley Subglacial Trench

Whitmore Mts.

Amundsen Sea

Beardmore Glacier

Whillans Glacier

Ross Ice Shelf

Dry Valleys

Mt. Erebus

Sulzberger Ice Shelf

Ross Sea

Ross Island

Onyx River

Lake Vanda

Roosevelt Island

INDIAN OCEAN

McMurdo Sound

Rennick Glacier

TRANSANTARCTIC MOUNTAINS

South Magnetic Pole 2013

Elevations in Antarctica

Feet	Meters
Over 10,000	Over 3,050
5,001–10,000	1,526–3,050
2,001–5,000	611–1,525
1,001–2,000	306–610
501–1,000	153–305
0–500	0–152

▲ Mountain peak

◄ Antarctic Circumpolar Convergence

0   500   1,000 miles
0   500   1,000 kilometers

Azimuthal Equal-Area Projection

SOUTHERN OCEAN

PACIFIC OCEAN

AUSTRALIA

PHYSICAL MAP OF ANTARCTICA

Not all of Antarctica is covered in snow and ice. Katabatic winds have rippled the rock and soil in the Wright Valley, one of the continent's Dry Valleys.

Transantarctic Mountains and the Ross Sea. The location of the mountains and strong winds prevent snow from falling in the Dry Valleys. In fact, no snow has fallen there in about 2 million years.

The narrow, mountainous Antarctic Peninsula is also part of West Antarctica. The peninsula extends farther north than any other part of the continent. This location gives the peninsula warmer temperatures and larger amounts of melting snow. Glaciers and an ice sheet cover the Antarctic Peninsula, though.

Lakes, Rivers, and Coasts

Most of Antarctica's lakes and rivers remain frozen year-round. Scientists have found about 145 freshwater lakes near the coast of East Antarctica. These lakes lie under the thick ice sheet, though. Using special instruments and tests, scientists discovered open water beneath the ice. They think that geothermal warming—heat from within the Earth— prevents the water from freezing.

In the summer, water appears in a few rivers and lakes in the Dry Valleys. The Onyx River receives freshwater from a melting glacier on West Antarctica's coast. As Antarctica's longest river, the Onyx flows 20 miles (32 km) inland into Lake Vanda in the Dry Valleys. Lake Vanda's

Lake Vostok

Lake Vostok is Antarctica's largest freshwater lake. It lies under about 14,000 feet (4,300 m) of ice on the Antarctic Plateau. Beneath the ice, Russian scientists from the Vostok Station discovered one of the world's largest volumes of open fresh water. They think that the water under the ice is more than one million years old. Lake Vostok could also have the world's cleanest, least polluted water.

In 1998, Russian scientists drilled an ice core from the lake. That ice was up to 400,000 years old. They stopped drilling before they reached the lake's water. The scientists did not want to pollute it. In 2012, scientists finally drilled through the ice into the water. They took special precautions to make sure that their tools would not contaminate the water. In 2013, the scientists found evidence that about 3,500 plants and animals, such as fungi, fish, and worms, live in Lake Vostok.

In East Antarctica, fog covers the Amery Ice Shelf that was formed by Lambert Glacier.

bottom water is salty, but freshwater from the Onyx stays at the top of the lake. The other lakes in the Dry Valleys are salt lakes.

Antarctica's coast is lined with large areas of ice shelves. They are formed when ice sheets or glaciers move onto the sea. Ice shelves remain attached to the ice sheet or glacier on land. In East Antarctica, the Lambert Glacier—the world's largest one—formed the Amery Ice Shelf. Antarctica's largest ice shelf is the Ross Ice Shelf, which is almost the size of Texas. Its icy cliffs stand 200 feet (60 m) above the Ross Sea.

When an ice shelf breaks from land, it becomes an iceberg. Only 10 percent of an iceberg is above water. In 2002, the huge Larsen B ice shelf broke off into the Weddell Sea. This piece of ice covered 1,049 square miles (2,717 sq km). That is about the size of the state of Rhode Island.

In the winter, **sea ice** forms when water from the surrounding ocean freezes. Attached to the coast and the ice shelves, the sea ice continues to grow. By the end of the winter, the sea ice has more than doubled the size of Antarctica.

Getting the Lay of the Land

Study the physical map of Antarctica on page 15 to answer the following questions:

1. What area of Antarctica extends north of the Antarctic Circle?

2. In which general direction does the Antarctic Circumpolar Convergence flow?

3. What major landform has Antarctica's highest elevations?

4. What major landform separates the Antarctic Plateau from the rest of Antarctica?

5. Which part of Antarctica has the largest ice shelves?

THREE

EARTH'S COLDEST, DRIEST, WINDIEST PLACE

Located south of the Equator, Antarctica is in the Southern Hemisphere. Australia and part of Africa and South America are also in that **hemisphere**. North America and Europe and most of Asia are in the Northern Hemisphere. The seasons occur differently on the continents in those two hemispheres. For example, Antarctica's summers begin in December and its winters start in June.

Climate regions are also arranged differently on continents in the two hemispheres. In Antarctica, temperatures are coldest farthest south, an area that lies in the middle of the continent. At Antarctica's northern edges, temperatures are just a bit warmer. In the Northern Hemisphere, temperatures are coldest in the north and become much warmer in the south.

20

Why Is Antarctica So Cold, Dry, and Windy?

Scientists drill an ice core sample from a wall of ice on Ross Island. They will use the sample to learn about changes in Antarctica's climate.

Antarctica's size, location, and elevation help make it the coldest, driest, and windiest continent.

Antarctica is a large, isolated landmass with a high elevation. The cold waters of the Southern Ocean swirl around it. Inland, Antarctica is higher in the center of the continent than at the coast. The coldest temperatures are found at those high elevations. Russia's Vostok Station on the Antarctic Plateau has Earth's lowest recorded temperature. In July 1983, the temperature plunged to minus 128.6 °F (-89.2°C).

Antarctica's position in relation to the sun adds to its low temperatures. The sun does not rise over Antarctica during most of the fall and all of the winter months. In that darkness, Antarctica receives little of the sun's warmth. Average low winter temperatures can reach minus 94°F (-70°C).

21

In the summer and most of the spring, the sun does not set. During this constant day, the ice and snow reflect most of the sun's light away from the land. That prevents the snow and ice from melting. The thick layers of snow and ice remain cold and frozen. In summer, temperatures mainly stay below freezing, which is 32°F (0°C). The continent's highest recorded temperature was 59°F (15°C). This occurred at New Zealand's Vanda Station in the Dry Valleys in May 1974.

Antarctica's fierce winds are created when cold air from the center of the continent races downhill to the coast. The winds become strongest at the coast. In fact, some of the world's strongest winds were clocked at 233 miles (375 km) per hour near France's Dumont d'Urville Station.

The combination of cold ocean water and cold winds prevents warmer, moister air from reaching into the continent. Inland, it is usually just too cold for snow to fall. Antarctica's lowest annual snowfall—0.08 inches (0.2 cm)—occurs at the US Amundsen-Scott South Pole Station. The most snow falls along the coast at an average of only 8 inches (20 cm) a year. Such low annual precipitation makes the entire continent a desert.

Causes of Climate Change in Antarctica

Major differences in temperatures and precipitation over several years are known as climate change. On the other continents, climate change has been caused by the activities of billions of people. Through thousands of years, they have emitted large amounts of CO_2 by burning coal, oil, and wood. In comparison, few people have ever been to Antarctica. Even now, only a few scientists and tourists can spend short amounts of time in Antarctica. Yet, evidence of climate change is found throughout the continent.

People on the world's other continents caused that change. Some products used by people throughout the world give off CFCs. Those gases caused thinning of the ozone layer over Antarctica. The ozone layer protects Earth from the sun's harmful ultraviolet (UV) rays. During the summer, the South Pole receives more direct radiation from the sun than any other place on Earth. Now, through the thinning ozone layer, more of the sun's ultraviolet (UV) rays hit Antarctica. UV rays have already damaged some Antarctic plants and animals.

The Southern Lights – Aurora Australis

In the Northern Hemisphere, colorful light displays occur in the winter near the Arctic Circle. These displays are called the aurora borealis, or northern lights. Because Antarctica is in the Southern Hemisphere within the Antarctic Circle, these strange winter lights are called the aurora australis, or southern lights. During the long Antarctic winter night, curtains of green, purple, or red light swirl through the sky. The lights are caused by particles in solar winds that have been caught by Earth's magnetic field.

Results of Climate Change

During the past 100 years, the other continents have experienced climate change. For example, the world's average temperature has increased about 1.3°F (0.74°C). Climate information in Antarctica has only been collected for the past 50 years. During that time, overall temperatures in parts of East Antarctica have dropped. In the winter, larger areas of sea ice form along the eastern coast.

Temperatures on the Antarctic Peninsula, however, have increased by about 5.4°F (3°C). Winter temperatures there are up by 9°F (5°C). This is the fastest rate of warming in the world. The Southern Ocean has warmed by about 1.8°F (1°C). It is warming faster than the world's other oceans.

The warming temperatures have affected the environment of the Antarctic Peninsula. More snow falls there in the winter, and some rain now falls in the spring. Glaciers on the peninsula are melting at faster rates. Large pieces of ice shelves are breaking off more often. Less sea ice forms along the peninsula in the winter.

Natural Disasters

Antarctica does not experience the natural disasters that occur on the other continents. Cyclones, hurricanes, and tornadoes do not happen there. Instead, **katabatic** winds cause blizzards that can lead to dangerous whiteouts. As the winds blow down from the Antarctic Plateau, they pick up snow that is already on the ground. The swirling snow creates a whiteout. People can barely see more than a few inches (cm)

How Scientists Measure Climate Change

Scientists conduct an experiment on the effects of global warming on the exposed Antarctic soil.

Throughout Antarctica, scientists use many methods to measure climate change. One method is drilling cores from the thick ice sheets. From the cores, scientists study the amounts of CO_2 that have been trapped in air bubbles in the ice. In 2004, French scientists drilled a core of ice that is about 800,000 years old. Air bubbles with CO_2 were found trapped in the ice. These bubbles tell how temperatures have changed throughout thousands of years. Other scientists on huge ships called icebreakers study Antarctica's ice shelves. They discovered that the air and water temperatures are warming, causing ice at the shelves' edges to melt.

Scientists also study fossils of plants that once grew in Antarctica. A fossilized fern tree stands upright between mountains on the Antarctic Peninsula. This shows that at one time Antarctica was warm and moist. Other scientists observe changes in animal behavior. For example, because the northern part of the Antarctic Peninsula has become warmer, fewer Adélie penguins are returning there.

The Adélie penguins stopped just in time at the edge of the crevasse.

in front of them. If people cannot find their way back to camp or to the research station during a whiteout, they could die.

Crevasses—long, deep cracks in the ice sheet— can also lead to disaster. These cracks are everywhere in Antarctica. Snow bridges build up over the crevasses, but they will not support people or vehicles. Because snow bridges are hard to detect, people have fallen through them into crevasses. Most of them died because they had fallen too far for rescuers to reach them.

Volcanic eruptions are another kind of natural disaster. Antarctica's main volcanoes are on Deception Island and Ross Island. Deception Island's volcano is underwater. Between 1967 and 1970, several eruptions occurred there that destroyed some research buildings. Heat from the volcano now warms the water in the island's bays. Visitors put on swimsuits and sit in the water even though the volcano could erupt again at any time.

Mount Erebus

Mount Erebus is an active volcano. It stands 12,447 feet (3,791 m) above sea level on Ross Island in the Ross Sea. Mount Erebus lies farther south than any of the world's other active volcanoes. The slopes of Mount Erebus are covered by glaciers. Temperatures there can plunge as low as -76°F (-60°C) in the winter. Inside the volcano, a lake of **lava** can get as hot as 2,066°F (1,130°C).

Mount Erebus's last major eruption occurred in 2006. This volcano continues to spew hot gases and lava bombs. That does not keep scientists away, though. They learn more about volcanoes as they climb the slopes of and explore ice caves inside Mount Erebus.

FOUR

A CHANGING NATURAL ENVIRONMENT

A harsh climate and rocky, ice-covered land support few plants and animals in Antarctica. Several animal species live on the continent only in spring and summer. A few simple plants also sprout up in the warmer months. In recent years, climate change has affected the habitats of many of these plants and animals. Human activities threaten some species.

Plants and Animals on Land

All of Antarctica is a cold desert. As is true in all deserts, some plants and animals manage to survive in Antarctica. In the spring, the continent's warmer coast supports algae, lichens, and mosses. In the Dry Valleys, mosses and lichens also grow inside rocks. The rocks protect these plants from the wind and cold. Throughout Antarctica, red, pink, green, and yellow algae grow on icy snow. The landscape looks like giant snow cones. Warm, moist conditions on the Antarctic Peninsula support Antarctic hair grass and Antarctic pearlwort. These are Antarctica's only flowering plants. Recent warming on the peninsula enables larger amounts of those plants to flourish.

Many scientists believe that algae bloom in Antarctica because of intense sunlight and the materials in the runoff from melting snow.

Several species of insects inhabit Antarctica. The wingless midge is the largest Antarctic insect, but it is only one-half inch (1 cm) long. Fleas, lice, and mites are other insects. Mites eat wingless midges, as well as algae and mosses. Another insect is the springtail. It feeds on algae near penguin colonies.

South Polar skuas will aggressively defend their territory.

Antarctica's only completely land-based birds are snowy sheathbills. They eat penguin eggs or penguin chicks that did not survive. Snow petrels and South Polar skuas are the most-southerly breeding birds. In the spring, snow petrels lay eggs in cracks high in Antarctica's eastern mountains. South Polar skuas lay eggs among rocks near Antarctica's coasts. Petrels and skua catch fish and krill for their young. None of these birds remain in Antarctica during the winter, though.

Humpback whales can grow to be more than 50 feet (15 m) long and can weigh up to 96,000 pounds (43,456 kg).

Life in the Sea

Water temperatures in the Southern Ocean are a bit warmer than temperatures on Antarctica's land. Many plants and animals live in that ocean's waters. In the winter, plankton and algae grow under the sea ice. Krill, small shrimplike animals, feed on these plants. In turn, birds, fish, seals, and whales depend on krill as their main food.

Fish in the Southern Ocean include the huge Antarctic cod, dragon fish, ice fish, and plunder fish. The blood of these fish contains a special protein that prevents them from freezing. Antarctic cod and ice fish have been overfished. Few of them remain. The Antarctic Treaty now strictly limits fishing in coastal waters.

Several species of seabirds glide over the Southern Ocean. They include cormorants, gulls, terns, and wandering albatrosses. They spend most of their lives in the air, but then they rest on the tops of ocean waves. When they are hungry, they swoop down and catch fish and squid. Sometimes these birds get caught up in hooks, lines, and nets set out by large fishing ships.

Whales are Antarctica's largest sea animals. In the summer, baleen whales—blue, humpback, and minke—feast on krill. These whales have no teeth. Instead, they have baleen plates that strain the krill from the water that they gulp. Orcas and sperm whales have teeth and they prey on seals and squid. In the winter, all the whales swim north to warmer waters to breed and raise their young. At one time, whales were overhunted. Now whale hunting is forbidden, and the number of whales is increasing. Today, the biggest dangers to whales are accidentally getting tangled in fishing nets or being hit by large ships.

Life on the Ice Shelves

Seals and penguins are the largest animals that spend time on Antarctica's ice shelves. Several species of seals live in nearby waters. Most of them eat krill, fish, and squid. In the spring, the seals move onto the ice shelves and have their pups. Then they teach the pups how to catch krill. Elephant seals are the world's largest seals. They live far north on the Antarctic Peninsula. Ross seals are the smallest Antarctic seals and live in the Ross Sea. Leopard seals are white with black spots and are found all around Antarctica's icy shores. They eat krill, fish, penguins, and other seals—mainly crabeater pups. Crabeater seals actually just eat krill. In the winter, Weddell seals live underwater, mainly in the Weddell Sea. They make holes in the ice and come up for air about once an hour.

Five species of penguins live in Antarctica—Adélie, chinstrap, emperor, Gentoo, and macaroni penguins. They breed and hatch and raise their young on ice near the coasts. On the ice, they waddle, hop, and slide. These birds do not fly. Instead, they use their wings as flippers for swimming. Penguins spend about 75 percent of their lives in the ocean. They feed on krill and fish.

Emperor penguins are the largest penguins. They can stay underwater longer than any other bird—about 20 minutes. They are also the only penguins that remain in Antarctica year-round. Emperors breed and hatch in Antarctica during the winter. The female emperor lays one egg at the beginning of winter. She heads out to sea to feed. The egg rests on the male emperor's feet under a warm fold of skin. In the spring, the female returns in time for the egg to hatch. To feed the new chick, she **regurgitates** the krill and fish that she ate at sea.

The emperor penguin is feeding her young chick by regurgitating food into its mouth.

The other species collect stones to build nests. In the early spring, they lay two eggs in their nests. Within a few months, those eggs hatch. Then the penguins must raise the chicks and teach them how to swim and fish on their own before the winter sets in. The penguins must also watch out for birds that feed on penguin eggs and on young chicks.

The thinning ozone layer and a warmer climate have resulted in less sea ice around the Antarctic Peninsula. Less sea ice means less plankton and algae for krill to eat. A smaller krill population means less food for penguins, seals, and whales. Today, fewer Adélie penguins breed on the Antarctic Peninsula. Large Adélie populations are still found along East Antarctica's coast. Currently, the biggest threats to Antarctica's penguins are raiding birds and leopard seals.

Where the Penguins Are

Several places on the Antarctic Peninsula have large colonies of penguins. In the summer, tourists from cruise ships watch these quirky birds. The penguins almost look like dolphins as they dive and resurface. A few lucky visitors might see a small group of emperor penguins, even though most of those penguins live in East Antarctica. For many years, scientists on the peninsula have studied large groups of "tuxedocd" Adélie penguins. Now, Adélie penguins find the peninsula too warm. Chinstrap, Gentoo, and macaroni penguins are taking the Adélie penguins' place. For these newcomers, the peninsula feels cool. The islands to the north where they had lived had become too warm.

FIVE

PEOPLE AND CHANGE

For more than two thousand years, scientists were sure that there was a continent at the "Bottom of the World." In the 1700s, explorers began sailing close to Antarctica. Finally in 1840, explorers proved that Antarctica was one large landmass—a continent. Large numbers of people did not rush to Antarctica, though.

Antarctica's Changing Population

For humans, Antarctica's cold, dry climate; ice-covered land; and long, dark winter provide harsh living conditions. That is why Antarctica has no permanent residents. In Antarctica, everyone is considered a visitor—scientists and their support staffs, as well as tourists.

Antarctica's population changes with the seasons. During the summer, about 4,400 scientists and support staff work at about 45 research stations. The scientists study climate change, measure glacial melting, drill ice cores, study rocks in the Dry Valleys, measure temperatures in the Southern Ocean, and observe changes in plants and animals. A research station's support staff might include cooks, doctors, and mechanics. They take care of people and equipment, such as vehicles, power stations, and laboratory tools.

Between 25,000 and 35,000 tourists also visit Antarctica each summer. They arrive on cruise ships. Zodiacs, small rubber boats, take them ashore. To cause

Antarctica's First People

In the early 1900s, explorers arrived from Britain and Norway and went ashore. They raced to be the first people to reach the South Pole. In 1909, a British team found the location of the magnetic South Pole. This is where the bottom of a compass needle points. In December 1911, Roald Amundsen's team from Norway reached the geographic South Pole. A few weeks later, Robert Scott and his British team arrived. Scott and his team did not return home. They died from cold and hunger on the Ross Ice Shelf. Today, small huts built by Scott and other explorers still stand on Ross Island. People who visit the huts learn about the hardships those men endured.

less damage to the environment, only 100 tourists can come ashore at the same time. Most of them stay only a few hours. Other tourists stay longer. They camp in special tents, hike on glaciers, or climb mountains. Both kinds of tourists must follow strict rules to protect the environment. For example, they cannot leave any waste, trample plants, or get too close to penguins.

In the winter, Antarctica's population decreases to about 1,000. A few support staff "winterover" to maintain the stations during the long, cold, dark winter. A few scientists "winterover" too. Some of them are astronomers. Antarctica's long, clear, dark night provides the perfect conditions to study the sky and space. Some stations completely close during the winter.

Where People Stay in Antarctica

Most people in Antarctica stay along the coast. That is where their countries have built the largest number of research stations. Many stations stand along the coast of East Antarctica, at the tip of the Antarctic Peninsula, and on Ross Island. Milder temperatures make the coast a good place to build research stations. Plus, they can be built more easily there. More time and money are required to transport food, equipment, and building supplies farther inland.

The coast of the Antarctic Peninsula and that of Ross Island are also the main areas visited by tourists. Along those shores, sea ice breaks up earlier each spring. Cruise ships can therefore more easily put people ashore.

Built in 1911 by explorer Robert F. Scott, "Scott's Hut" was abandoned in 1917. Today it stands as a reminder of the harsh conditions faced by Antarctica's explorers in the early 1900s.

Only a few countries have built stations inland. The US South Pole Station is the farthest inland. Russia's Vostok Station is also far inland in East Antarctica.

During the summer, some scientists conduct research in the field— away from the research stations. Much of that research takes place far inland. The scientists camp out in tents built to withstand Antarctica's strong winds that carry stinging, blowing ice.

McMurdo Station

The US McMurdo Station was built on Ross Island's volcanic rock. It's not from Mount Erebus. McMurdo accounts for 25 percent of Antarctica's summer and winter populations. About 1,000 scientists and support staff work there in the summer. About 250 people remain through the winter.

With more than 100 buildings, McMurdo is the largest research station in Antarctica. It is almost like a small town. Besides having scientific laboratories and living quarters for everyone, McMurdo has an airport, a hospital, a church, a library, and restaurants. Some of the

staff publish a newspaper or broadcast programs from local radio stations. Other staff members cook meals, raise vegetables in a greenhouse, collect garbage and waste materials, or repair equipment and vehicles.

The people at McMurdo try to take care of Antarctica's environment. Their water plant removes salt from seawater to provide the station's water supply. Heat created from this water process provides safe fuel to warm the station's buildings. Wind turbines generate some of McMurdo's electricity.

SIX

LOOKING FOR SOLUTIONS TO PRESENT-DAY PROBLEMS

Antarctica is the only continent that has not been carved into separate countries. Instead, about 25 percent of the world's countries have agreed to protect Antarctica. They have also pledged to share the results of scientific research gained from their scientists on the continent. Through their work, Antarctica has become Earth's largest laboratory.

Antarctica's Major Problems

Even though no permanent residents live in Antarctica, population is becoming a problem. Research stations continue to be built. More scientists and support staff come to work at them. In addition, larger numbers of tourists visit Antarctica every year. Each person adds stress to the continent's environment. For example, both research station workers and tourists have accidentally brought alien insects and plant seeds to

The orange portions of the map show areas with warming temperatures. Since 1958, the average annual temperature of West Antarctica has risen the most, 4.3°F (2.4°C).

Antarctica. These materials were stuck in their boot treads or in Velcro closures. With warming temperatures, some of these alien species could grow and overtake Antarctica's native plants and animals.

The major problem facing Antarctica is climate change. Scientists predict that by 2100 Antarctica will have warmer temperatures and more snowfall. This is expected to occur in both winter and summer across the continent. Warmer temperatures would speed up melting of glaciers and ice sheets. If melting occurs at the current rate, sea levels could rise 20 inches (50 cm). If all of Antarctica's ice sheets were to melt, the sea level rise could be more than 260 feet (80 m). If that happened, cities along the coasts on all the other continents would be underwater.

Other problems include the thinning ozone layer over Antarctica and methane under the ice sheets. After the thinning ozone layer was discovered in 1985, many governments agreed to stop using CFCs. In recent years, the thin ozone area has been improving. By 2050, scientists think the ozone layer will be back to normal. Now scientists fear that if the ice sheets melt, billions of tons of methane may escape. Before ice covered Antarctica, decay from large plants and animals created methane. Release of methane will add to warming, melting, and sea level rise.

Toward a Better Tomorrow

Even with its problems, Antarctica still has Earth's cleanest environment. In many ways, the continent is Earth's greatest natural resource. First, Antarctica's ice and snow acts like a giant air conditioner for Earth. The whiteness and cold of the ice reflect the sun's rays away from Earth. Second, about 75 percent of Earth's freshwater is frozen in Antarctica's ice. Scientists are studying ways to tow icebergs to areas of the world suffering from water shortages. Melting from icebergs and ice shelves will not add to sea level rise. That ice is already part of the ocean. Third, the cold water of the Southern Ocean naturally absorbs CO_2. Scientists are studying ways to increase this absorption. Then, the warming temperatures on land and ocean surfaces would decrease.

Countries with activities in Antarctica are working to protect the environment. They have agreed not to mine any of the continent's natural resources. Deposits of coal, copper, iron ore, gold, nickel, and platinum are trapped deep below Antarctica's ice. Mining them would ruin the natural environment. Most countries are working to reduce the use of CO_2-emitting fuels at their research stations. Now, electricity at some stations is also created from solar power and wind energy.

In 2041, the ban on mining in Antarctica will expire. Scientists and other people hope that the world's countries will renew that part of the Antarctic Treaty. Antarctica deserves the continued protection of countries on Earth's other six continents.

Princess Elisabeth Station

In 2009, Belgium opened Princess Elisabeth Antarctica Station. This station is on the opposite side of the continent from the US McMurdo Station. Princess Elisabeth was the first zero-emission station on the continent. It emits no CO_2 and is completely powered by solar panels and wind turbines. Between 25 and 40 people work in the station's one building—and only in the summer. The steel building looks like a spaceship standing on stilts that are pushed deep into the rocks.

GLOSSARY

Antarctic Circumpolar Current
the ocean current that flows around Antarctica, keeping water from warm oceans away from the continent

chlorofluorocarbon
a gas given off by aerosol sprays and by coolants in refrigerators and air conditioners, causing thinning of the ozone layer

climate change
an increase or decrease in temperature or rainfall over a long period of time

continent
a large land mass

crevasse
a long, deep crack in a glacier or in an ice sheet

glacier
a long, wide sheet of thick, slowly moving ice and snow

habitat
the place in which a plant or animal lives

hemisphere
one half of Earth, such as the Eastern, Northern, Southern, or Western hemisphere

iceberg	an ice shelf that has broken off from the land or part of an ice shelf that has broken off
ice sheet	thick ice that completely covers a large area of land
ice shelf	a large area of floating ice that is attached to land; originally part of an ice sheet or glacier
katabatic	winds that blow down from the Antarctic Plateau, causing blizzards and whiteouts
lava	hot, liquid rock that can flow or be thrown from a volcano
methane	a gas given off from animal waste, decaying plants, and garbage
ozone layer	a layer of gas that protects Earth from the sun's harmful ultraviolet (UV) rays
regurgitate	to pull partly digested food up from the stomach and back into the mouth
sea ice	ice that forms when ocean water freezes
tectonic plates	the hard sheets of moving rock that make up Earth's crust
tsunami	a huge, damaging wave caused by an underwater earthquake

FIND OUT MORE

BOOKS

Britton, Arthur K. *Life at a Polar Research Station*. Extreme Jobs in Extreme Places. New York: Gareth Stevens Publishing, 2013.

Latta, Sara L. *Ice Scientist: Careers in the Frozen Antarctic*. Berkeley Heights, New Jersey: Enslow Publishers, 2009.

Taylor, Barbara. *Arctic and Antarctic: Discover the Polar Regions and the Remarkable Plants and Animals that Survive Here*. DK Eyewitness Books. London: DK, 2012.

Walker, Sally M. *Frozen Secrets: Antarctica Revealed*. Minneapolis, Minnesota: Carolrhoda Books, 2010.

DVDS

Antarctica: An Adventure of a Different Nature. Museum of Science and Industry/ MagicPlay Entertainment.

Globe Trekker—Antarctica & South Atlantic. Pilot Productions, 2010.

WEBSITES

National Science Foundation—US South Pole Station
http://www.nsf.gov/news/
Besides information about the South Pole Station, the links provided take you to webcams from all three US research stations and to *The Antarctic Sun*, the US online newspaper. When harsh weather conditions limit live webcam viewing during Antarctica's winters, tapes of the aurora australis are shown.

Discovering Antarctica
http://www.discoveringantarctica.org.uk/
This British website presents tons of information through fact sheets, video clips, and photos. British explorations of Antarctica are thoroughly covered, also.

INDEX

ABOUT THE AUTHOR

Patricia K. Kummer has a B.A. in history from St. Catherine University in St. Paul, Minnesota, and an M.A. in history from Marquette University in Milwaukee, Wisconsin. She has written chapters for several world history and American history textbooks and has authored more than sixty books about countries, states, natural wonders, inventions, and other topics. Books she has written for Cavendish Square include *Working Horses* in the Horses! series and the seven books in the Climates and Continents series.